P9-DEL-170

TRY iT WiTH FOOD!

Children's Press®
An Imprint of Scholastic Inc.
New York   Toronto London   Auckland Sydney
Mexico City   New Delhi   Hong Kong
Danbury, Connecticut

Book production: Educational Reference Publishing

Book design: Nancy Hamlen D'Ambrosio

Science adviser: Jennifer A. Roth, M.A.

Library of Congress Cataloging-in-Publication Data

Try it with food.
    p. cm. — (Experiment with science)
  Includes bibliographical references and index.
ISBN-13: 978-0-531-18544-5 (lib. bdg.)   978-0-531-18761-6 (pbk.)
ISBN-10: 0-531-18544-3 (lib. bdg.)   0-531-18761-6 (pbk.)
  1. Science—Experiments—Juvenile literature. 2.
Food—Experiments—Juvenile literature. I. Children's Press (New York,
N.Y.) II. Title.
 Q164.T79 2008
 507.8—dc22
                                    2007020446

All rights reserved. Published by Children's Press, an imprint of Scholastic Inc.
Printed in China. 62

3 4 5 6 7 8 9 10 R 17 16 15 14 13 12 11 10

CONTENTS

TRY iT WiTH FooD!

Most of us think of the kitchen as that special room where we prepare and eat food. But to the scientist, the kitchen is also a great laboratory. It's a place to experiment with food. In its most basic form, food is a group of chemicals—chemicals that have come together to produce a special taste and to look a certain way. The nutrients in food—carbohydrates, fats, proteins, vitamins, and minerals—are necessary for the cell and tissue growth that keeps our bones strong, our hearts pumping, and our brains functioning.

Each experiment in this book leads you through the steps you must take to reach a successful conclusion based on scientific results. There are also important symbols you should recognize before you begin your experiment. Here's how the experiments are organized:

Name of experiment

Goal, or purpose, of the experiment

A **You Will Need** box provides a list of supplies you'll need to complete the experiment, as well as the approximate amount of time the experiment should take.

Here's What You Will Do gives step-by-step instructions for working through the experiment.

Here's What's Happening explains the science behind the experiment—and what the conclusion should be.

Mess Factor shows you on a scale of 0 to 5 just how messy the experiment might be (a good thing to know before you begin!).

MESS FACTOR: 3

Science Safety: Whenever you see this caution symbol, read the instructions and be extra careful.

It's also important to remember that food is like a fuel. Our bodies run on food just as cars run on gasoline and flashlights run on batteries. Food gives your body the energy it needs to run, to play, to work, or to just enjoy life. And as an ingredient in a science experiment, food has many things going for it. For starters, just about everything you'll need is right at your fingertips. Can you think of a better place to test and measure and experiment than in your own kitchen? And when else is it okay to nibble on your work?

Look around your kitchen: the ingredients for your experiments are everywhere: in the refrigerator, in the cabinet, in the breadbox. In this book, we'll use all sorts of foods: lemons and apples, rice and cereal, peas and butter—even hot dogs. So wash your hands, put on an apron, and double-check your grocery list. The first experiment is only as far away as your kitchen!

This symbol means that you should ask an adult to help you or be nearby as you conduct the experiment. Although all the experiments in this book are appropriate and safe for kids to do, whenever you're handling anything that might be sharp or hot, it's important to have adult supervision.

ADULT

In the back of the book, **Find Out More** offers suggestions of other books to read on the subject of food, and cool Web sites to check out. The **Glossary** (pages 30-31) provides definitions of the highlighted words appearing throughout this book. Finally, the **Index** is the place to go to find exactly what you're looking for.

Here are some important tips before you begin your experiment:

- Check with an adult.
- Read the experiment all the way through.
- Gather everything you need.
- Choose and prepare your "lab" work area.
- Wash and dry your hands.
- Use only clean containers for your experiments.
- Keep careful notes of everything you do and see.
- Stop and ask an adult if you aren't sure what to do.
- When you're finished, clean up your work area completely, and wash your hands!

METAL FOR BREAKFAST?

WE ALL NEED IRON IN OUR DIET. IN THIS EXPERIMENT, YOU'LL USE A BAR MAGNET TO DRAW OUT TINY IRON FILINGS FROM FORTIFIED BREAKFAST CEREAL.

Don't just pump iron—eat it! Iron is one of the most important metals that we humans need in our diet for good health.

YOU WILL NEED

- ❑ 1 cup Total™ brand cereal
- ❑ quart-size zipper-lock plastic bag
- ❑ measuring cup
- ❑ about 2 cups warm water
- ❑ bar magnet

TIME: 45 MINUTES

MESS FACTOR: 3

HERE'S WHAT YOU WILL DO

Pour the cereal into the bag. Seal the bag and squish it to crush the flakes into a powder.

Open the bag and fill it halfway with warm water. Seal it again. Leave some air inside. But make sure you have a watertight seal!

Hold one end of the magnet against the outside of the bag while you gently slosh the cereal "soup" against it. Keep sloshing slowly and gently. Be patient.

Do you see something dark forming on the inside of the bag near your magnet? Pull your magnet away. Does the spot disappear? Try it again.

HERE'S WHAT'S HAPPENING

We humans need small amounts of metals such as iron, magnesium, zinc, and chromium in our diet for good health. Iron ranks among the most important of these. So you'll find this metal in multivitamins and in many fortified foods. In this experiment, your magnet is attracting tiny iron filings from the fortified cereal. If at first you don't see results, let your cereal sit for half an hour. This will allow more iron to separate from the crushed flakes.

ELECTRIC LEMON

IN THIS EXPERIMENT, YOU'LL USE A LEMON TO MAKE AN ELECTRICAL CURRENT JUST STRONG ENOUGH TO GIVE YOUR TONGUE A TINGLE.

A battery is a device that produces electrical energy. It is the most common portable source of power.

YOU WILL NEED

- ❑ 1 fresh lemon
- ❑ butter knife
- ❑ 2 steel paper clips
- ❑ 1 penny
- ❑ 1 nickel

TIME: 15 MINUTES

MESS FACTOR: 1

HERE'S WHAT YOU WiLL DO

Squeeze the lemon between your hands—enough to soften it but not to break the skin. Use the butter knife to carefully cut two slits in the lemon about ½ inch (1.25 centimeters) apart.

Straighten out the paper clips. Insert one paper clip "wire" about ½ inch into each slit. Push a coin in each slit alongside the wire. Make sure that each wire is snug against its coin.

Touch the opposite ends of both wires to your tongue. What do you feel? Pull one wire away from your tongue. Does the sensation stop?

HERE'S WHAT'S HAPPENING

The tingle you feel is a very small amount of electricity. Together, the lemon, the coins, and the wires form a simple battery. Inside your battery, an acid (the lemon juice) carries electricity between two electrodes made of different metals—in this case, nickel and copper. When both wires touch your tongue, they complete an electrical circuit, so the current flows out of the battery, through your tongue, and back to the battery again.

CRAZY COLLOIDS

CREATE A COLORFUL COLLOID, JUST LIKE QUICKSAND! AND DEMONSTRATE SOME OF THE FASCINATING FACTS ABOUT WHAT'S A SOLID AND WHAT'S A LIQUID.

Quicksand is found most often in valleys, bogs, and riverbeds or streambeds. In this mountain gorge, sediment at the bottom of the stream mixes with water to create quicksand.

 YOU WILL NEED

- ❑ measuring cup
- ❑ 1 cup cornstarch
- ❑ large bowl
- ❑ 1/2 cup water
- ❑ food coloring

TIME: 30 MINUTES

MESS FACTOR: 5

HERE'S WHAT YOU WiLL DO

t 1 cup of cornstarch into the bowl. the measuring cup with ½ cup of ater. Add a few drops of food loring.

Slowly add the water to the corn- arch while squishing and stirring gether the mixture with your nds. Continue mixing for three or four inutes.

Grab a big handful of the goop and squeeze *ARD!* Does it feel solid? Now open your hand, lm up. Does it turn back to a squishy goop?

Next, try pushing your finger *slowly and ntly* into the mixture. Is it easy to push rough? Try poking it hard and fast. Is it more fficult to push through?

Try rolling the goop between your hands until forms a ball. Then stop and let the ball melt vay again. What else can you do with this eird stuff?

ANSWER THiS!

If you had one leg stuck in quicksand, would it be easier to pull it out slowly or quickly?

See next page to find out why.

[Answer: Slowly!]

REMEMBER THIS....

When it comes to handling colloids, think **slow for flow**.

HERE'S WHAT'S HAPPENING

Have you ever seen quicksand in a nature show or read about it in a book? People or animals that get stuck in quicksand have a hard time getting out! Quicksand is a natural example of a colloid—a unique substance that's both solid and liquid at the same time! When you mix cornstarch and water together, the cornstarch only seems to dissolve. In reality, its tiny solid particles hang suspended in the water. In the same way, very fine sand can become suspended in water to form a pit of quicksand. If you press hard against a colloid, you meet resistance, because the floating particles can't get out of the way fast enough. Push slowly, and they slip aside.

FANTASTIC FUNGI

TRY THIS FUN-GI EXPERIMENT, AND GROW A WILD AND WEIRD GARDEN THAT DEMONSTRATES THE ABUNDANCE OF INVISIBLE MOLD SPORES IN ORDINARY AIR.

YOU WILL NEED

- leftovers (bread, pasta, cheese, fruit, vegetables, etc.)
- small amount of water
- glass jar with screw-on lid
- magnifying glass (optional)

TIME: 2 WEEKS

ADULT

MESS FACTOR: 2

It's not difficult to imagine that the mold on this loaf of bread is a living organism. Mold is a fungus that feasts on moist, decaying things.

△
Safety First!
Some people are very allergic to mold. So keep your jar tightly closed. And have an adult dispose of your "garden" by emptying it into a bag and sealing it.

HERE'S WHAT YOU WILL DO

1 Tear the leftovers into small chunks (about the size of a quarter). Dampen them with a little water.

2 Place the open jar on its side. Spread out the food inside, and screw the lid on tight. (Leave the jar on its side.)

3 Find a warmish spot (room temperature is fine) where you can leave your "garden-in-a-jar" undisturbed for a couple of weeks.

4 Check back each day or two and record what you see. Take a closer look with a magnifying glass.

GOURMET MOLD!

Though we usually think of moldy food as "spoiled," cheese makers use special molds to make flavorful products. The blue-green fungus *Penicillium roqueforti*, for example, gives us both Roquefort and blue cheese (above).

before mold sets in

after mold sets in

HERE'S WHAT'S HAPPENING

We know that all living things come from other living things. However, some organisms reproduce using eggs and spores too small to see with the naked eye.

Mold is a kind of fungus. It grows from dustlike spores that float all around us. Moisture encourages mold spores to sprout from their dormant, or "sleeping," state. In this experiment, you probably have several kinds of mold in your jar. Do some look fuzzy? The threadlike tangles are spore stalks. Each holds one or more tiny spore cases filled with thousands of new spores ready to fly out into the air.

MUMMY MADNESS

THIS CREEPY EXPERIMENT WILL DEMONSTRATE HOW PEOPLE THROUGHOUT HISTORY HAVE USED DESICCANTS—MINERALS THAT ABSORB MOISTURE—TO PRESERVE FOOD AND, YES, EVEN THEIR DEAD.

This Egyptian mummy is the body of a human that was preserved after death. The most important step in mummification was dehydration—the removal of all moisture from the body.

YOU WILL NEED

- ❑ 2 cups baking soda
- ❑ 2 cups salt
- ❑ small box or plastic container
- ❑ small apple
- ❑ potato peeler
- ❑ hot dog
- ❑ black marker

TIME: 1 WEEK

MESS FACTOR: 1

HERE'S WHAT YOU WILL DO

Pour the baking soda and salt in a container that will be just big enough to hold the apple and hot dog. Mix well.

Use the potato peeler to remove the apple's skin and carve a face into the apple. The peeler's tip works well for gouging out eyes and nostrils.

Using your marker, draw a fake fingernail on one end of the hot dog (as if it were a fat finger). Bury the apple and hot dog in the soda-salt mixture, and leave them for a full week. Unbury them and take a look!

HERE'S WHAT'S HAPPENING

Have you ever wondered how the Egyptians made mummies? Or how some ancient people shrank the heads of their dead enemies? This experiment shows you how. You ended up with your own "shrunken head" and "mummy finger" because the baking soda and salt drew the water out of both the apple and the hot dog. Drying food (or bodies) causes them to shrink because they are made mostly of water. It also keeps them from spoiling because the molds and bacteria that normally decompose dead matter need water to grow.

SEEING SOUND

HAVE YOU EVER FELT A LOUD NOISE? IN THIS EXPERIMENT, YOU'LL SEE THE POWER OF SOUND ENERGY AND DEMONSTRATE HOW SOUND WAVES TRAVEL THROUGH THE AIR.

A tuning fork is a piece of metal that vibrates when hit. You can see the vibration of sound when you put the tuning fork in a glass of water—the water vibrates!

YOU WILL NEED

- ❏ plastic cling wrap
- ❏ large bowl
- ❏ measuring cup
- ❏ 1/4 cup uncooked rice
- ❏ metal pot
- ❏ large metal spoon
- ❏ rubber band (optional)

TIME: 15 MINUTES

MESS FACTOR: 1

HERE'S WHAT YOU WILL DO

1. Stretch the plastic wrap over the bowl so that you have a tight fit. If the plastic won't stick, use a rubber band to hold it tightly across the bowl.

2. Scatter rice grains across the stretched plastic.

3. Hold the opening of your pot near the rice's "dance floor." Bang loudly on the back of the pot with the spoon. What does the rice do each time you hit the pot?

HERE'S WHAT'S HAPPENING

Sound is a kind of vibration that pushes air in front of it, creating invisible waves. Each time a sound wave hits the plastic wrap, the wrap wiggles and the rice jumps. In this same way, sound hits your eardrums. You hear the sound because the nerves in your ears turn the vibration into electrical signals that travel to your brain. Your brain interprets, or understands, the electrical signals as sound.

OFF TO THE RACES!

PLEASE PLAY WITH YOUR FOOD! IN THIS EXPERIMENT, YOU'LL DEMONSTRATE THE SCIENTIFIC PRINCIPLE OF CONDUCTIVITY AND LEARN WHAT KINDS OF MATERIALS ARE BETTER CONDUCTORS THAN OTHERS.

Steel is an excellent conductor of heat. This steelworker is softening a metal rod by heating it so that it can be shaped.

 YOU WILL NEED

- ❑ 1 teaspoon slightly firm butter
- ❑ 3 dried or frozen peas
- ❑ large wooden serving spoon
- ❑ large metal serving spoon
- ❑ large plastic serving spoon
- ❑ large mug or measuring cup
- ❑ adult helper
- ❑ very hot water

TIME: 20 MINUTES

 MESS FACTOR: 1

 ADULT

HERE'S WHAT YOU WILL DO

1 Use a small piece of the butter to stick a pea to the stem of each spoon, several inches up from the bowl end of the spoon. To run a fair race, keep the size of the butter pieces and their distance from the end of the spoons about the same.

2 Place the spoons in the mug. Keep their stems apart.

3 Have an adult add very hot water to the mug. Which pea slides down the stem of the spoon first?

HERE'S WHAT'S HAPPENING

Metals are good conductors. That means that they allow energy to pass through them easily. So heat—a form of energy—travels fastest up the metal spoon to melt the butter and send the pea sliding. Plastic and wood are poor conductors. Heat flows through them slowly. But that makes them good insulators.

iNFLATiON CREATiON

HOW CAN YOU INFLATE A BALLOON WITHOUT BLOWING INTO IT OR USING A PUMP? IN FINDING THE ANSWER, YOU'LL DEMONSTRATE WHAT HAPPENS WHEN AN ACID AND A BASE MIX.

Baking soda is one ingredient that makes cakes increase in volume. This cake has 75 layers and is over 21 feet (6.5 meters) high!

YOU WiLL NEED

- ☐ funnel
- ☐ empty single-serving glass soda bottle
- ☐ 1 cup white vinegar
- ☐ spoon
- ☐ 4 tablespoons baking soda
- ☐ balloon

TIME: 20 MINUTES

MESS FACTOR: 3

HERE'S WHAT YOU WILL DO

Use the funnel to fill the soda bottle a third full with vinegar.

Next, funnel several heaping spoonfuls of baking soda into the deflated balloon.

Slip the opening of the balloon onto the neck of the bottle. Make sure you have a tight seal.

Lift the balloon so that the baking soda empties into the bottle. Now stand back and watch!

HERE'S WHAT'S HAPPENING

This amazing experiment is simple chemistry! The baking soda is a compound that is a base, and the vinegar is an acid. When they meet, they react to form lots of bubbles and new compounds, including enough carbon dioxide gas to inflate your balloon.

BAKING BUBBLES

Baking soda is often an ingredient in cakes and cookies. The bubbles it produces give the batter or dough a light and fluffy texture and help it increase in volume.

BENDY BONES AND BOUNCY EGGS

WHAT WOULD HAPPEN IF THE CALCIUM IN YOUR BONES (OR A BIRD'S EGGSHELL) WERE TO SUDDENLY DISAPPEAR? FIND OUT IN THIS EXPERIMENT.

Milk and green leafy vegetables are rich in calcium. Calcium is a mineral that helps build strong teeth and bones.

YOU WILL NEED

- ❑ 2 hard-boiled eggs (un-peeled)
- ❑ cleaned and dried wing bones from cooked chicken
- ❑ 2 glass jars
- ❑ 2-3 cups white vinegar
- ❑ 2-3 cups water

TIME: 3-5 DAYS

MESS FACTOR: 1

HERE'S WHAT YOU WILL DO

Put one hard-boiled egg and half the bones in one jar. Cover them with vinegar.

Put the other egg and bones in the second jar. Cover them with water. Leave the eggs and bones to soak for three to five days.

Fish the egg and bones out of the vinegar. How do they feel? Can you bend the bones or bounce the egg? Do the same with the egg and bones soaked in water. How do they feel?

CALCIUM, YES! SODA... NO!

Foods rich in calcium, such as milk and leafy green vegetables, help build strong teeth and bones. But studies show that the acid in soft drinks weakens tooth enamel and bones. So health experts urge kids of all ages to avoid colas and lemon-lime sodas. Reach for milk and soy drinks instead!

HERE'S WHAT'S HAPPENING

There's a good reason to be sure you get enough **calcium** in your diet. Without this important mineral, your bones can become weak and brittle. Bones and eggshells are both rich in the **mineral** calcium. In this experiment, the vinegar, which is an **acid**, dissolved most of the calcium. And the eggshells became soft and bouncy. Water had no effect at all on the strength of the bones or the eggshells. The result of this experiment shows how important calcium is in our diets.

GELATIN OPTICS

GET "JIGGLY" WITH IT IN THIS EXPERIMENT AND MAK
SOME COLORFUL GELATIN "GLASSES." TRY THEM ON TO
DEMONSTRATE THE PRINCIPLES OF MAGNIFICATION
AND REFRACTION.

A magnifying glass is a convex lens that makes
objects look bigger than they really are.

YOU WILL NEED

- ❑ 1 box lemon-flavored gelatin
- ❑ 4-cup Pyrex measuring cup
- ❑ adult helper
- ❑ 1 cup boiling water
- ❑ stirring spoon
- ❑ assortment of small containers (glass, plastic, or metal measuring cups, spoons, saucers)
- ❑ clear, flat lid or plate

TIME:
5 HOURS

MESS FACTOR:
2

HERE'S WHAT YOU WiLL DO

1 Empty the box of gelatin into the Pyrex measuring cup. Ask an adult to slowly pour the hot water into the bowl as you stir. Keep stirring until the gelatin is completely dissolved.

2 Let the mixture cool for five minutes. Then pour some into your small containers, which are your molds.

3 Carefully put the containers in the refrigerator so that they don't spill.

4 After four hours, remove the molds from the fridge. Turn them upside down on a clear lid or plate. (The plastic lid from a deli container or a glass pie plate works well.) If the gelatin doesn't plop out easily, dip the bottom of the containers into warm water to loosen the gelatin.

5 Look through your gelatin "lenses" at objects, pictures, and the pages of this book. Does the size of the lens affect the magnification? Does the magnification change when you move the lens closer or farther away from what you're looking at?

HERE'S WHAT'S HAPPENING

Have you ever wondered how a magnifying glass makes objects look bigger than they are? The curved surface of a convex lens causes the light passing through it to spread out, or refract, on its way to your eye. As a result, you see an image that appears bigger than it really is. Larger lenses produce greater magnification, as does increasing the distance from the object being magnified.

In this experiment, your gelatin "magnifying glasses" also magnify objects. The amount of magnification depends on the size and shape of the gelatin mold.

CONCAVE OR CONVEX?

If an object is curved like the inside of a bowl, it is called concave. People often use concave mirrors to magnify their faces when applying makeup or shaving. Convex surfaces, such as the underside of this spoon, are shaped like the outside of a bowl. They cannot produce a magnified image, but they enable you to see a wider view. Passenger-side mirrors on cars are usually convex.

FIND OUT MORE

For more information on the science of food, check out these books and Web sites:

BOOKS

Dispezio, Michael. *Awesome Experiments in Electricity and Magnetism.* Sterling, 1999.

Fletcher, Joann, and John Malam. *Mummies: And the Secrets of Ancient Egypt.* Dorling Kindersley, 2001.

Gardner, Robert. *Science Projects about Sound.* Enslow, 2000.

Goldstein, Margaret J., and Barbara Beirne. *Household History: Eyeglasses.* Lerner, 1997.

Llewellyn, Claire. *Material World: Plastics.* Scholastic, 2001.

Nankivell-Aston, Sally, and Dorothy Jackson. *Science Experiments with Electricity.* Watts, 2000.

Pascoe, Elaine. *Slime, Molds, and Fungi (*Nature Close-up Series). Thomson Gale, 1998.

Royston, Angela. *Body Needs: Vitamins and Minerals for a Healthy Body.* Heinemann, 2003.

Zoehfeld, Kathleen Weidner, and Paul Meisel. *What Is the World Made Of?: All about Solids, Liquids, and Gases.* Turtleback Books, 1998.

WEB SITES

Encyclopedia Smithsonian: Egyptian Mummies
www.si.edu/resource/faq/nmnh/mummies.htm
Learn about the process of mummification that was common in ancient Egypt. From the Smithsonian.

Exploratorium: Science Snacks about Electricity
www.exploratorium.edu/snacks/iconelectricity.html
Start your own electric flea circus or make a magnetic field that's stronger than the Earth's. These are just two experiments at this site having to do with electricity!

From Lenses to Optical Instruments
www.funsci.com/fun3_en/lens/lens.htm
These simple experiments with lenses teach how optical instruments (such as telescopes and microscopes) work. From Fun Science Gallery, an award-winning Web site aimed at amateur scientists of any age.

MyPyramid.gov—USDA—For Kids
www.mypyramid.gov/kids/index.html
The food pyramid is one way for people to understand how to eat healthy. These food pyramid materials for kids are by the U.S. Department of Agriculture.

Sound Site
www.smm.org/sound
Close your eyes and open your ears! Find activities, sound cards, and multimedia explorations about sound.

WonderNet—Chemical Reactions
www.chemistry.org/portal/a/c/s/1/wondernet display.html?DOC=wondernet\activities\react\ reactions.html
One of the neat things about chemicals is the way they can break apart and join together in new ways to form different chemicals. Try some fun activities at this Web site from the American Chemical Society.

WonderNet—Polymers
www.chemistry.org/portal/a/c/s/1/wondernet display.html?DOC=wondernet\activities\polymers\ polymers.html
Polymers are long chains of chemicals found almost everywhere in nature. Some polymers, such as plastic, can also be made in factories. To learn more about polymers, try some fun activities at this American Chemical Society site.

GLOSSARY

A

acid a substance that will react with a base to form a salt. Examples of acid substances are lemon juice and vinegar.

B

bacteria simple, one-celled organisms; the oldest and most common form of life on Earth.

base a substance that will react with an acid to form a salt. Examples of base substances are ammonia and dish detergent.

battery a device that stores energy and makes it available as electricity.

C

calcium a mineral that gives strength to bones, teeth, and shells.

carbon dioxide a colorless and odorless gas that is a mixture of carbon and oxygen.

chemistry the scientific study of substances, what they are made of, and the ways in which they react with each other.

chromium a chemical element that is a hard silvery-gray metal.

circuit the complete path that an electrical current can flow around.

colloid a mixture of solid particles suspended in a liquid. The particles in paints, gelatins, and many other colloids do not dissolve, but remain suspended for long periods of time.

compound something formed by combining two or more parts.

concave curving inward, like the inside of a bowl.

conductivity the ability or power to conduct heat, electricity, or sound.

conductors substances that allow heat, electricity, or sound to travel through them.

convex curving outward, like the outside of a bowl.

current the movement of electricity through a wire.

D

decompose to rot or decay.

desiccants minerals that absorb moisture.

dormant not active for a time, as if asleep.

E

eardrums thin tissue, or membranes, in the ear that vibrate in response to sound.

electrodes posts or wires that conduct electricity, or allow electricity to pass, into or out of a device.

enamel the hard white surface of your teeth.

energy power, or the ability to make something change or move. Forms of energy include light, heat, and electricity.

F

filings particles or shavings of metal.

fortified enriched with vitamins and minerals to increase nutritional value.

fungus an organism that resembles a plant, but has no leaves, flowers, or roots. Fungi (the plural of fungus) include molds, yeasts, and mushrooms. They extract their food from living or dead matter.

G

gas a substance, such as air, that will spread to fill any space that contains it.

I

insulators substances that resist the passage of energy; insulators help keep warm things warm, and cold things cold.

iron a metal that is found in some foods and in your body's red blood cells. Iron helps transport oxygen in the blood.

L

liquid one of three states of matter; liquids flow and take the shape of their containers.

M

magnesium a light silver-white metal. It is often used in making fireworks.

magnification making something look bigger than it is.

metals chemical elements that are good conductors of heat and electricity.

mineral a substance found in nature that is not an animal or a plant. Gold, salt, and copper are all examples of minerals.

molds filmy or fuzzy fungi (the plural of fungus) that grow on damp or decaying surfaces.

N

nerves cells that convey messages to the brain.

O

organisms living plants or animals.

P

preserve to protect something so that it stays in its original state

Q

quicksand loose, wet sand that heavy objects can sink into.

R

refraction the bending of light as it passes from one clear substance into another of a different density.

resistance a force that opposes the motion of an object.

S

solid a state of matter with a definite shape and volume.

sound wave a traveling vibration perceived as sound when it strikes the ear.

soy the soybean plant. Soybeans are a good source of protein and oil.

spores plant cells that develop into a new plant. Spores are produced by plants that do not flower, such as fungi (the plural of fungus), mosses, and ferns.

suspended kept from falling as if attached from above.

V

vibration a rapid back-and-forth motion.

Z

zinc a blue-white metal. It is often used to coat other metals so that they will not rust.

iNDEX

Pictures are shown in **bold**.

Photographs © 2008: Alamy Images: 8 (Adams Picture Library), 3 top left, 6 (Stock Image/Pixland); AP Images: 4 center right, 22 (Hermann J. Knippertz); Corbis Images: 4 center, 14 bottom left (Jean Pierre Fizet/Sygma), 5 center left, 20 (John Madere); fabfoodpix.com: 1; Getty Images/David Toase: 13; JupiterImages: 24 (Radius Images), 26 (Chip Simons); Photo Researchers: 4 left, 16 (Richard T. Nowitz), 10 (Bernhard Edmaier/Science Photo Library), 5 center right, 18, 28 bottom (Andrew Lambert Photography/Science Photo Library); Richard Hutchings Photography: front cover, back cover, 3 bottom left, 3 center left, 3 top right, 3 center right, 4 right, 4 center left, 5 right, 5 center, 5 left, 7, 9, 11, 12, 14 top right, 15 top right, 15 left, 17, 19, 21, 23 top, 25 top right, 27 top, 27 left, 28 top, 29 top right; StockFood, Inc./Peter Hogg/Food Image Source: 23 bottom.